British Library Cataloguing in Publication Data

Nichols, Grace
 Come on into my tropical garden.
 I. Title   II. Binch, Caroline
 811   PZ8.3

 ISBN 0–7136–2989–4

Text © 1988 Grace Nichols
Illustrations © 1988 Caroline Binch

Published by A & C Black (Publishers) Ltd
35 Bedford Row, London WC1R 4JH

Filmset by August Filmsetting, Haydock, St Helens
Printed by Netherwood Dalton & Co Ltd, Huddersfield

Come on into my Tropical Garden

Grace Nichols

Illustrated by Caroline Binch

A & C Black · London

Contents

Come on into my Tropical Garden

Come on into my tropical garden
Come on in and have a laugh in
Taste my sugar cake and my pine drink
Come on in please come on in

And yes you can stand up in my hammock
and breeze out in my trees
you can pick my hibiscus
and kiss my chimpanzees

O you can roll up in the grass
and if you pick up a flea
I'll take you down for a quick dip-wash
in the sea
believe me there's nothing better
for getting rid of a flea
than having a quick dip-wash in the sea

Come on into my tropical garden
Come on in please come on in

3

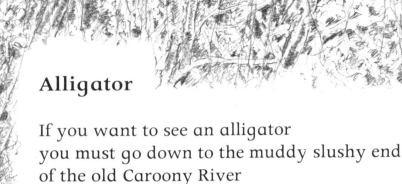

Alligator

If you want to see an alligator
you must go down to the muddy slushy end
of the old Caroony River

I know an alligator
who's living down there
She's a-big. She's a-mean. She's a-wild.
She's a-fierce.

But if you really want to see an alligator
you must go down to the muddy slushy end
of the old Caroony River

Go down gently to that river and say
'Alligator Mama
Alligator Mama
Alligator Mamaaaaaaaa'

And up she'll rise
but don't stick around
RUN FOR YOUR LIFE

5

I Like to Stay Up

I like to stay up
and listen
when big people talking
jumbie stories

I does feel
so tingly and excited
inside me

But when my mother say
'Girl, time for bed'

Then is when
I does feel a dread

Then is when
I does jump into me bed

Then is when
I does cover up
from me feet to me head

Then is when
I does wish I didn't listen
to no stupid jumbie story

Then is when
I does wish I did read
me book instead

('Jumbie' is a Guyanese word for 'ghost')

They Were my People

They were those who cut cane
to the rhythm of the sunbeat

They were those who carried cane
to the rhythm of the sunbeat

They were those who crushed cane
to the rhythm of the sunbeat

They were women weeding, carrying babies
to the rhythm of the sunbeat

They were my people working so hard
to the rhythm of the sunbeat

They were my people, working so hard
to the rhythm of the sunbeat – long ago
to the rhythm of the sunbeat

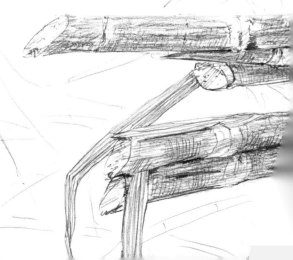

Poor Grandma

Why this child
so spin-spin spin-spin
Why this child
can't keep still

Why this child
so turn-round
turn-round
Why this child
can't settle down

Why this child
can't eat without getting
up to look through window
Why this child must behave so
I want to know
Why this child
so spin-spin spin-spin
Why this child
can't keep still

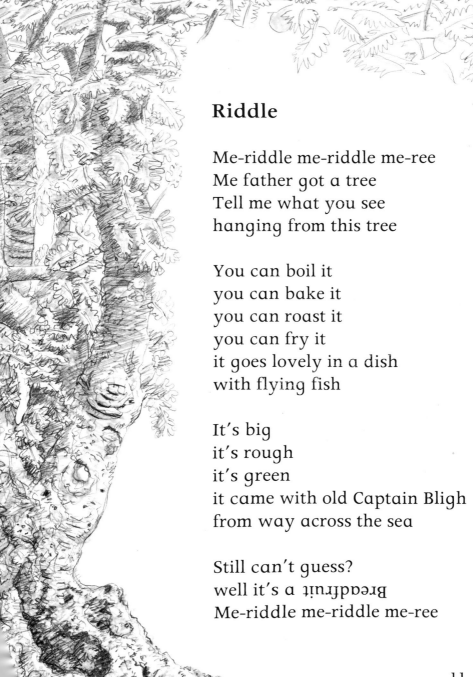

Riddle

Me-riddle me-riddle me-ree
Me father got a tree
Tell me what you see
hanging from this tree

You can boil it
you can bake it
you can roast it
you can fry it
it goes lovely in a dish
with flying fish

It's big
it's rough
it's green
it came with old Captain Bligh
from way across the sea

Still can't guess?
well it's a Breadfruit
Me-riddle me-riddle me-ree

11

Granny Granny Please Comb my Hair

Granny Granny please comb
my hair
you always take your time
you always take such care

You put me on a cushion
between your knees
you rub a little coconut oil
parting gentle as a breeze

Mummy Mummy
she's always in a hurry-hurry
rush
she pulls my hair
sometimes she tugs

But Granny
you have all the time
in the world
and when you're finished
you always turn my head and say
'Now who's a nice girl'

My Cousin Melda

My Cousin Melda
she don't make fun
she ain't afraid of anyone
even mosquitoes
when they bite her
she does bite them back
and say –
'Now tell me, how you like that?'

Wha Me Mudder Do

Mek me tell you wha me Mudder do
wha me mudder do
wha me mudder do

Me mudder pound plantain mek fufu
Me mudder catch crab mek calaloo stew

Mek me tell you wha me mudder do
wha me mudder do
wha me mudder do

Me mudder beat hammer
Me mudder turn screw
she paint chair red
then she paint it blue

Mek me tell you wha me mudder do
wha me mudder do
wha me mudder do

Me mudder chase bad-cow
with one 'Shoo'
she paddle down river
in she own canoe
Ain't have nothing
dat me mudder can't do
Ain't have nothing
dat me mudder can't do

Mek me tell you

The Fastest Belt in Town

Ma Bella was the fastest belt in town
Ma Bella was the fastest belt
for miles and miles around

In fact Ma Bella was the fastest belt
both in the East and in the West
nobody dared to put Ma Bella to the test

plai-plai
her belt would fly
who don't hear must cry

Milk on the floor
and Ma Bella reaching for – de belt

Slamming the door
and Ma Bella reaching for – de belt

Scribbling on the wall
and Ma Bella reaching for – de belt

Too much back-chat
and yes, Ma Bella reaching for – de belt

plai-plul
her belt would fly
who don't hear must cry

Ma Bella was the fastest belt in town
Ma Bella was the fastest belt
for miles and miles around

In fact Ma Bella was the fastest belt
both in the East and in the West
nobody dared to put Ma Bella to the test

Until one day
Ma Bella swished
missed
and lashed her own leg

That was the day Ma Bella got such a welt
That was the day Ma Bella knew exactly how it felt
That was the day Ma Bella decided to hang up her belt.

Moody Mister Sometimish

Mister Sometimish, Mister Sometimish
you too sometimish!

Sometimish you tipping you cap
with a smile

Sometimish you making you face
sour like lime

Sometimish you stopping in for a chat
Sometimish you passing just like that

Sometimish you saying 'how-dee' and you waving
Sometimish you putting your head straight
you playing you ain't hearing
when I calling you
but Mister Sometimish I can be sometimish too
because you too sometimish, Mister Sometimish
Man you too sometimish.

19

Mango

Have a mango
sweet rainwashed
sunripe mango
that the birds themselves
woulda pick
if only they had seen it
a rosy miracle
Here
take it from mih hand

Banana Man

I'm a banana man
I just love shaking
those yellow hands
Yes, man
Banana in the morning
Banana in the evening
Banana before I go to bed
at night – that's right
that's how much I love
the banana bite

I'm a banana man
not a superman
or a batman
or a spiderman
No, man
Banana in the morning
Banana in the evening
Banana before I go to bed
at night – that's right
that's how much I love
the banana bite

Drinking Water-coconut

Feeling thirsty
feeling hot
nothing to cool you down
like a water-coconut

With a flick of her cutlass
market-lady will hand you one –
a sweet little hole brimming at the top
when you put it to yuh head
you wouldn't want it to stop

Then you'll be wondering
if there's jelly inside
ask market-lady she wouldn't mind
she'll flick the big nut right open for you
she'll flick you a coconut spoon
to scoop with too

Feeling thirsty
feeling hot
the best thing to spend yuh money on
is a water-coconut

Early Country Village Morning

Cocks crowing
Hens knowing
later they will cluck
their laying song

Houses stirring
a donkey clip-clopping
the first market bus
comes jugging along

Soon the sun
will give a big yawn
and open her eye
pushing the last bit of darkness
out of the sky

24

The Sun

The sun is a glowing spider
that crawls out
from under the earth
to make her way across the sky
warming and weaving
with her bright old fingers
of light

25

Sky

Tall and blue
true and open

So open my arms have room
for all the world
for sun and moon
      for birds and stars

Yet how I wish I had the chance
to come drifting down to earth –
      a simple bed sheet
covering some little girl or boy
just for a night
      but I am Sky
      that's why

I am the Rain

I am the rain
I like to play games
like sometimes
        I pretend
I'm going
        to fall
Man that's the time
I don't come at all

Like sometimes
I get these laughing stitches
up my sides
        rushing people in
and out
        with the clothesline
I just love drip
            dropping
down collars
            and spines
Maybe it's a shame
but it's the only way
I get some fame

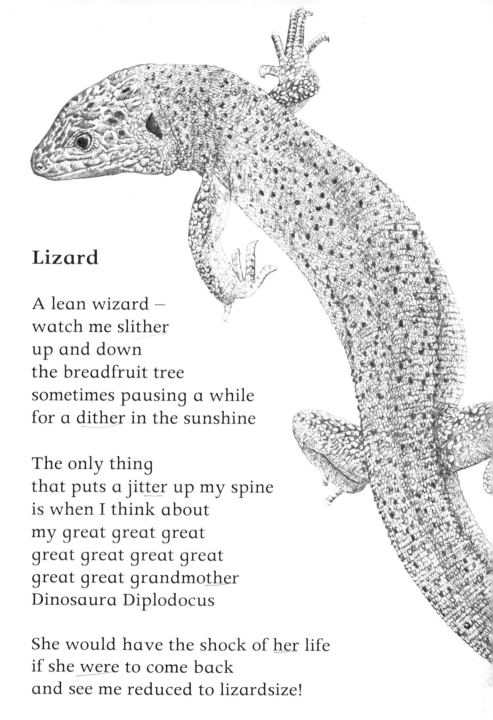

Lizard

A lean wizard –
watch me slither
up and down
the breadfruit tree
sometimes pausing a while
for a dither in the sunshine

The only thing
that puts a jitter up my spine
is when I think about
my great great great
great great great great
great great grandmother
Dinosaura Diplodocus

She would have the shock of her life
if she were to come back
and see me reduced to lizardsize!

Dinosaurs

Diplodocus
Brontosaurus
Tyrannosaurus
Fabrosaurus

How I love the sound of dinosaurs
even though they were supposed to be
big and ugly and made wars

Dinosaurs O Dinosaurs
you might have been ferocious
but what a loss!

One hundred million years ago
you were the boss

Cow's Complaint

Somebody calls somebody
a lazy cow
now in my cow's life
I ask you how?

If it wasn't so unfair
I would have to laugh
Dear children, as it is
I can only ask

Who gives you the milk
for your cornflakes
(crispy crunchy yes)
but it's my nice cold milk

that really brings them awake
children make no mistake

Who gets up at the crack of dawn
and works until the set of sun
Who eats up the grass
helping to mow the place for free
tell me who if it isn't me

Who gives you hamburgers
Who gives you steaks
it's my meat they take
it's my meat they take

So the next time
you call anyone a lazy cow
think again, my friend, you'd better
especially if your shoes are made of leather

Old Man's Weary Thoughts

Sun — too much sun
Rain — too much rain
Grass — too much green
Sky — too much blue
'Lord, dis world
ah weigh me down fuh true!'

I'm a Parrot

I am a parrot
I live in a cage
I'm nearly always
in a vex-up rage

I used to fly
all light and free
in the luscious green
forest canopy

I am a parrot
I live in a cage
I'm nearly always
in a vex-up rage

I miss the wind
against my wing
I miss the nut
and the fruit picking

34

I am a parrot
I live in a cage
I'm nearly always
in a vex-up rage

I squawk I talk
I curse I swear
I repeat the things
I shouldn't hear

So don't come near me
or put out your hand
because I'll pick you
if I can
pickyou
pickyou
if I can

I want to be Free
Can't You Understand

Parakeets

Parakeets wheel
       screech
          scream
in a flash of green
among the forest trees
sunlight smooth their feathers
cool leaves soothe their foreheads
creeks are there for beaks
lucky little parakeets

Doctor Blair

Doctor Blair is the name of a bat
down out in the forest
they call him that

Cause Doctor Blair has a flair
for visiting his patients in the dead of night
his little black sac tucked under his back
his scissors-sharp teeth and his surgical flaps

Even if you don't want to see him
Doctor Blair makes his rounds
and he comes without as much as a sound
to perform a pain free operation

In fact Doctor Blair works with such care
that you'll sleep through
in the morning all you'll see on your leg
is a little line of blue

Where the blood seeped through
Where the blood seeped through

*(Remembering Oliver Hunter, Guyana man and
one-time pork knocker who told me about Dr Blair)*

For Forest

Forest could keep secrets
Forest could keep secrets

Forest tune in every day
to watersound and birdsound
Forest letting her hair down
to the teeming creeping of her forest-ground

But Forest don't broadcast her business
no Forest cover her business down
from sky and fast-eye sun
and when night come
and darkness wrap her like a gown
Forest is a bad dream woman

Forest dreaming about mountain
and when earth was young
Forest dreaming of the caress of gold
Forest rootsing with mysterious Eldorado

and when howler monkey
wake her up with howl
Forest just stretch and stir
to a new day of sound

but coming back to secrets
Forest could keep secrets
Forest could keep secrets

And we must keep Forest

Sea Timeless Song

Hurricane come
and hurricane go
but sea — sea timeless
sea timeless
sea timeless
sea timeless
sea timeless

Hibiscus bloom
then dry wither so
but sea — sea timeless
sea timeless
sea timeless
sea timeless
sea timeless

Tourist come
and tourist go
but sea — sea timeless
sea timeless
sea timeless
sea timeless
sea timeless

Crab Dance

Play moonlight
and the red crabs dance
their scuttle-foot dance
on the mud-packed beach

Play moonlight
and the red crabs dance
their side-ways dance
to the soft-sea beat

Play moonlight
and the red crabs dance
their bulb-eye dance
their last crab dance